Crypto Coin Mining for Fun & Profit

Information and How to Guide to Crypto Coin Mining.

Making extra money with the use of a computer and the Internet.

By D. R. Gordon © 2017 All Rights Reserved

Version 1.02 DEC 2017

To My oldest son tells me that his friend had just sold most of his crypto currency for over $37,000 dollars and that he had only spent a couple months mining, when all the sudden they went from almost nothing to over $20 in value. I was overwhelmed and amazing and at the time didn't even understand what he was saying. I wanted to make money with my computer too and have a new way of making money that was 2015. I took the adventure of figuring out what mining was, how to do it and make a lot of money doing it. Many weeks of searching and studying the best possible information from all aspects and the processes of mining. I finally achieved the goal of mining coins for profit. After showing a good friend about my new venture, I quickly realized that people might also want this information that I have painstakingly compiled. So I put together the processes in a straight forward basic manner for people who have knowledge of basic computer skills could do this themselves. I would like to dedicate this book to my son.

A big thank you to him, for his unknowingly help and information into the creation of this book. Dad.

Follow Us : www.facebook.com/cyrptocurrency

What is Crypto Coin Currency?

Cryptocurrency is a digital medium of exchange. It has also been nicknamed Cryptocoin or even just the word Coin. The first Crypto Currency Coin to begin trading was Bitcoin in 2009. Since then, numerous crypto currencies have become available. Fundamentally, crypto currencies are specifications regarding the use of currency which seek to incorporate principles of cryptography to implement a distributed, decentralized and secure information economy. Peer-to-peer Internet currency that enables instant payments to anyone in the world. A crypto currency is a digital asset designed to work as a medium of exchange using cryptography to secure the transactions and to control the creation of additional units of the currency. Crypto currencies are a subset of alternative currencies, or specifically of digital currencies. Bitcoin became the first decentralized crypto currency in 2009. Since then, numerous crypto currencies have been created. These are frequently called altcoins, as a blend of bitcoin alternative. Bitcoin and its derivatives use decentralized control as opposed to centralized electronic money/centralized banking systems. The decentralized control is related to the use of Bitcoin's blockchain transaction database in the role of a distributed ledger.It is based on the Bitcoin protocol but differs from Bitcoin in that it can be efficiently mined with consumer-grade hardware. The blockchain is capable of handling higher transaction volume than its counterpart Bitcoin. Due to more frequent block generation, the network supports more transactions without a need to modify the software in the future. As a result, merchants get faster confirmation times, while still having ability to wait for more confirmations when selling bigger ticket items.

What is Crypto Coin Mining?

Mining is the term used to describe the process of extracting cryptocurrency tokens from a blockchain network and involves having computers continuously run a hashing algorithm, which takes an arbitrarily large amount of information and condenses it to a string of letters and numbers of a fixed length. The hashing algorithm hashes metadata from the most recent block using something called a nonce: a binary number that produces a unique hash value. For each new block in the blockchain, the network sets a target hash value and all the miners on the network try to guess the nonce that will result in that value. Mining is the process of adding transaction records to coin public ledger of past transactions. This ledger of past transactions is called the block chain as it is a chain of blocks. The block chain serves to confirm transactions to the rest of the network as having taken place nodes use the block chain to distinguish legitimate transactions from attempts to re-spend coins that have already been spent elsewhere. Mining is intentionally designed to be resource-intensive and difficult so that the number of blocks found each day by miners remains steady. Individual blocks must contain a proof of work to be considered valid. This proof of work is verified by other nodes each time they receive a block.

The primary purpose of mining is to allow nodes to reach a secure, tamper-resistant consensus. Mining is also the mechanism used to introduce coins into the system: Miners are paid any transaction fees as well as a "subsidy" of newly created coins. This both serves the purpose of disseminating new coins in a decentralized manner as well as motivating people to provide security for the system. Mining is so called because it resembles the mining of other commodities: it requires exertion and it slowly makes new currency available at a rate that resembles the rate at which commodities like gold are mined from the ground. These coins currently are most easiest of mining any others. The whole focus of mining is to accomplish three things: Provide bookkeeping services to the coin network. Mining is essentially 24/7 computer accounting called 'verifying transactions'. Get paid a small reward for your accounting services by receiving fractions of coins every couple of days. Keep your personal costs down, including electricity and hardware.

What does GPU Mean?

What does GPU mean? The Graphics Processing Unit, known as your Graphics Card or Video Card.The Speed of the Cards are in kH/s or kHps or kHash/s = kilohashes per second or the total hashing speed of all cores on the CPU or GPU.

Setting Reasonable Expectations

If your objective is to earn substantial money as a second income, then you are better off purchasing cryptocoins with cash instead of mining them, and then tucking them away in the hopes that they will jump in value like gold or silver bullion. If your objective is to make a few digital bucks and spend them somehow, then you just might have a slow way to do that with mining. Smart miners need to keep electricity costs to under $0.11 per kilowatt-hour; mining with 4 GPU video cards can net you around $8.00 to $10.00 per day (depending upon the crypto currency you choose), or around $250-$300 per month. AMD Radeon graphic processing units and the market value of crypto coins. Now, there is a small chance that your chosen digital currency will jump in value alongside Bitcoin at some point. Then, possibly, you could find yourself sitting on thousands of dollars in crypto coins.

Laundry List: What You Will Need

1. A private database called a coin wallet. This is a password-protected container that stores your earnings and keeps a network-wide ledger of transactions.
2. A free mining software package, like this one from AMD, typically made up of cgminer and stratum.
3. A membership in an online mining pool, which is a community of miners who combine their computers to increase profitability and income stability.
4. Membership at an online currency exchange, where you can exchange your virtual coins for conventional cash, and vice versa.
5. A reliable full-time internet connection, ideally 2 megabits per second or faster speed.
6. A hardware setup location in your basement or other cool and air-conditioned space.
7. A desktop or custom-built computer for mining. A separate dedicated computer is ideal. Tip: Do not use a laptop, gaming console or handheld device to mine. These devices just are not effective enough to generate income.
8. ATI graphics processing unit (GPU) or a specialized processing device called a mining ASIC chip. The cost will be anywhere from $90 used to $3000 new for each GPU or ASIC chip. The GPU or ASIC will be the workhorse of providing the accounting services and mining work.

9. A house fan to blow cool air across your mining computer. Mining generates substantial heat, and cooling the hardware is critical for your success.
10. Personal curiosity and appetite for reading and constant learning, as there are ongoing technology changes and new techniques for optimizing coin mining results. The most successful coin miners spend hours every week studying the best ways to adjust and improve their coin mining performance.

What is SHA-256, Scrypt, X11?

There were more than 710 crypto currencies available for trade in online markets as of 11 July 2016 and more than 760 now in total but only a few dozen had reached a market capitalization above $10 million above as of early 2017. Real time information such price or market capitalizations can be accessed at Crypto-Currency Market Capitalizations. This Book mainly with cover SHA-256, Scrypt coins. However there are currently:X11, Quark, Groestl, Blake-256 , NeoScrypt, Lyra2REv2, CryptoNight, EtHash and Equihash Hashing Methods. With several thousand cryptocurrencies in existence right now, it is not surprising to learn a lot of coins use different mining algorithms. Bitcoin uses SHA-256, other coins may use X11, Keccak, or Scrypt-N. These algorithms have their own benefits and requirements to keep mining competitive. Below are some of the different mining algorithms to be found today, and how they compare to one another.

Scrypt. Quite a few different alternative cryptocurrencies make use of the Scrypt mining algorithm. Scrypt was initially designed to make it costly to perform large-scale custom hardware attacks, as it requires large amounts of memory. However, cryptocurrencies such as Tenebrix and Litecoin use a simplified version of Scrypt Even though this may be a simplified version, the mining process still requires significant computing memory resources.

Even though the introduction of Scrypt meant dedicating bitcoin mining hardware – known as ASICs – could not be used, it did not take long for companies to start producing Scrypt ASICs. Moreover, powerful AMD graphics cards are more than capable of mining the Scrypt algorithm, even though they will draw a lot of electricity while doing so. Over the past few years, several hundred altcoins using the Scrypt algorithm have popped up, including the top ones Litecoin and Dogecoin.

It is worth noting there are other Scrypt mining algorithms, including Scrypt-N and Scrypt-Jane, each of which adds their own unique flavor. Scrypt-N for example, changes the memory requirement of the algorithm every set amount of time, this way even if ASICs are developed for the algorithm, a few years later they become obsolete as the "N" changes and creates the need for different circuits in order to mine the hashes. Furthermore, there is also the Scrypt-OG algorithm, which is 8 times less memory-intensive than Scrypt. In fact, the term "OG" stand for "Optimized for GPU".

X11. A new mining algorithm started to make some waves in the altcoin community in the year 2014. X11, as this algorithm is called uses 11 different rounds of hashes (hence the 11), was well received due to this incredibly energy-efficiency while mining with a GPU or

CPU. This algorithm is also capable of keeping mining hardware a lot cooler as there is a lower requirement for processing power. This effectiveness also translated into lower operation costs due to less electricity being used. Moreover, X11 prevented the use of existing ASICS – in 2014 – which allowed anyone with a semi-decent computer to mine X11-based cryptocurrencies. Unfortunately, the X11 algorithm did not prove to be ASIC-resistant for too long. Especially once popular cryptocurrency Dash – also known as XCoin and Darkcoin – embraced X11, it was only a matter of time until the first ASICs came to fruition. PinIdea and Baikal are two types of X11 ASIC miners which have become very common these days.Even though X11 ASICs have become more common, the algorithm remains a secure solution for cryptocurrency developers looking to thwart brute-force attacks.

It is worth mentioning the next iterations of this algorithm which are X13, X14, X15, and X17. As you might have guesses, X13 contains 13 rounds of hashes, X15 contains 15, and so forth. Through our research the highest X algorithm we found was X17 which was introduced back in 2014. Essentially if you look at the hash function below you will see the 17 hash functions that make up the X17 algorithm.

The new altcoins love boasting the fact that they use new algorithms in order to generate more profit and hype for the Cryptocurrency world.

SHA-256. The SHA-256 algorithm is used to mine Bitcoin, generating new addresses on the network and support the network through proof-of-work. It is worth noting SHA-256 is part of the SHA-2 cryptographic hash function initially designed by the NSA. In the early days of Bitcoin mining, it was feasible to use a powerful CPU. Once the mining software was modified to support graphic cards, GPUs became the new preferred form of mining hardware. Eventually, FPGAs and ASICs took over. y making use of these application-specific integrated circuits, mining Bitcoin has become a very expensive process. These machines require a lot of electricity, even though they have become more energy-efficient as of late. A different iteration of SHA-256, which goes by the name of SHA-256D, was conceived as well, which serves as a double SHA-256 cryptographic hashing algorithm

The following list of Cryptocurrencies are being compared to Bitcoin mining to determine if a cryptocurrency is more profitable to mine than mining Bitcoin. The cryptocurrency profitability information displayed is based on a statistical calculation using the hash rate values entered and does not account for difficulty and exchange rate fluctuations, stale/reject/orphan rates, a pool's efficiency, and pool fees. Your individual profitability may vary. Interest in these type of hashing and profit vs cost can be found at website:

www.coinwarz.com/cryptocurrency

The Cryptocurrency Top Four

1. Bitcoin   SHA-256

The first decentralized ledger currency. Crypto currency with the most famous, popular, notable and highest market capitalization Bitcoin has become a really valuable coin to have and use. Bitcoin has also become the main coin that is used to trade among the other coins. Most all exchanges and company who have wallets promote Bitcoin as top tier and purchases. Currently the markets have it set up to use Bitcoin and Etherium Coins for the main connection of an exchange. Usally you have to buy Bitcoin first then trade to other ones. For instance if you have some Doge Coins and want to trade some for Etherium coin. you will first have to trade/sell the Doge Coin for Bitcoin first then trade Bitccoin to Etherium Coin.

The main advantages of Bitcoins over other cryptocurrencies, according to Bitcoin developer and Medium writer Jimmy Song, are its network effect and proven security. According to him, other advantages of Bitcoins that make them unique are:
Bitcoin is more accessible with more merchants, more exchanges, and software/hardware support systems available. It has the largest developer ecosystem with more software and more implementations. First mover advantage: Large user base, loyalists, and entrepreneurs creating companies (open source projects, startups) around it.
It is far more liquid than other digital currencies. Security has been proven far more than its much younger counterparts with usage by almost every metric exceeding that of altcoins. It has a large lead as a store of value.

Hashing algorithm: SHA2
Stock Exchange Tag: BTC
Total Coins to Be Issued: 21 million
(approximately the year 2040)
Current Market Value Per Coin: ~$20000.00 USD

Pros: Highly recognized, can spike in value; extremely high profitability for the people that were early adopters in 2009.

Cons: The BTC double-spending glitch worries some people; extremely difficult to earn money as a miner unless you have expensive and server-level hardware; electricity cost is prohibitive if you do not have discount access to power. The value of BTC can also drop sharply.

Notes: Criminals gave Bitcoin a bad name in 2013 because BTC was used to move large volumes of illegal money on the Silk Road drug website. Similarly, the mismanagement of the Mt.Gox exchange service also gave the general public a fear around BTC trustworthiness when they lost many millions of dollars worth of customers Bit coins to "Hackers". Currently with better protection software.

2. Ethereum ETH

Like Bitcoin, Ethereum is a distributed public blockchain network. Although there are some significant technical differences between the two, the most important distinction to note is that Bitcoin and Ethereum differ substantially in purpose and capability. Bitcoin offers one particular application of blockchain technology, a peer to peer electronic cash system that enables online Bitcoin payments. While the Bitcoin blockchain is used to track ownership of digital currency (bitcoins), the Ethereum blockchain focuses on running the programming code of any decentralized application. In the Ethereum blockchain, instead of mining for bitcoin, miners work to earn Ether, a type of crypto token that fuels the network. Beyond a tradeable cryptocurrency, Ether is also used by application developers to pay for transaction fees and services on the Ethereum network.

3. Lightcoin   LTC

Hashing algorithm: Scrypt
Stock Exchange Tag: LTC
Total Coins to Be Issued: 82 million
Discovery Time for Each New Block: 2.5 minutes
Reward for Each New Block: 50 coins
Current Market Value Per Coin: ~$39.70 USD
Pros: Faster blockchain discovery rate, very possible for individual users to use consumer-level hardware to make a small income mining Litecoins; the larger cap on total coins will reduce the compulsion for people to hoard Litecoins.
Cons: You will need an AMD Radeon video card to mine Litecoins; GPU and nVidia hardware mining is not profitable
Notes: Litecoins were designed using Bitcoin code but with much faster algorithm confirmation and much more mining accessibility for consumers with personal computers.

4. Doge Coin   DOGE

Hashing algorithm: Scrypt
Stock Exchange Tag: DOGE
Total Coins to Be Issued: 100 billion
Discovery Time for Each New Block: 1 minute
Reward for Each New Block: 250 coins

Current Market Value Per 1000 Dogecoins: ~$2.53 USD
Pros: Designed to be a 'tipping' currency (high volumes of movement, low coin value); very easy for a user to mine with consumer-grade hardware; if you can keep the electricity costs down, Dogecoins can be a reliable small passive income for computer enthusiasts. Cons: You will need an AMD Radeon video card to mine Dogecoins; GPU and nVidia hardware mining is not profitable Notes: The pronunciation of 'Doge' is controversial. The coin itself is named after a dog meme; the mascot of Dogecoins is the Japanese Shiba Inu dog; Dogecoin miners are affectionally called 'Shibes'. Dogecoin uses Comic Sans MS font and bad English grammar as part of its identity.

Since its launch in December of 2009, Dogecoins have achieved remarkable market capitalization value on the stock exchange. There is a friendly appeal to this tipping currency, and it shows in how many people are participating in its mining and use. There are even free places on the Web called 'Doge faucets' that give away small amounts of Dogecoins for free.

Dogecoins became world famous during the winter Olympics in Sochi because Dogecoin donors sponsored the Jamaican bobsled team to the tune of $30,000 USD.

What is a Cryptocurrency Wallet?

A cryptocurrency wallet is a software program that stores private and public keys and interacts with various blockchain to enable users to send and receive digital currency and monitor their balance. If you want to use Bitcoin or any other cryptocurrency, you will need to have a digital wallet. A cryptocurrency coin wallet is a secure digital wallet used to store, send, and receive digital currency like Bitcoin. In order to use any cryptocurrency you will need to use a cryptocurrency wallet.

Desired Traits of a Wallet

What are the desired traits of a crypto wallet and how hard can choose a wallet to be?

Convenience may come at the cost of security; additional features may come at the cost of a steeper learning curve. More importantly you value over the others? Here are some suggested thing to think about when using a wallet.

1. Cost. Is it free? What are the drawbacks of using this wallet?
2. Security. Does the company have a track record of security excellence?
3. Mobility. Is it easy to keep and difficult to lose? Is it accessible anytime, anywhere?
4. User-friendliness. Is the wallet UI intuitively designed? Can I store a range of altcoins?
5. Convenience. Am I able to make a fast purchase when the time calls for it?
6. Style. Do I have a weakness for cool tech gadgets?

You may want a wallet that offers the best combination of the above-mentioned traits. Remember, all wallets have their different costs, performances, pros and cons.

KeepKey – Hardware Wallet.
Nano Ledger S – Hardware Wallet.
Trezor – Hardware Wallet.
Coinbase – Hot Wallet.
MyEtherWallet – Paper Wallet.
Jaxx — Software Wallet.

Electrum – Software Wallet.

Online Wallets Vs Paper Wallets

In the most specific sense, a paper wallet is a document containing all of the data necessary to generate any number of private keys, forming a wallet of keys. However, people often use the term to mean storing offline as a physical document. The paper wallets have QVR Codes that can be scanned as well as a unique serial code for manual input.

Coinbase is an American Company. Use this link and Purchase $100 get $10 USD.

www.coinbase.com/join/52b4cabe71b60773f9000071

Coinbase is a digital currency exchange and wallet holder, headquartered in San Francisco, California. They broker exchanges of Bitcoin, Ethereum, Litecoin and other digital assets with fiat currencies in 32 countries. Founded: 2012

When you sign up using your referral code you'll get 10% off discount on all trading fees for 6 months. Signup page URL: www.gate.io/signup/129542

Wallet Back Ups & Safe Storage

Visit the currency client website that you would like to have. you can search the name of the coin and find it online. Download wallet zip file to "download files folder" and then extract the client file to a 8 GB USB Flash Pen Drive that you place into usb port and formated ready to accept the client file. Open the Coin Currency Folder, and click on the file to open the client wallet program. Update the Payout name to you. Encrypt the passphrase and it will ask if ok then restart after you click yes. then restart and update client to current blocks date. always back up your wallet after updates and payouts. save to a folder named wallet back up.

1. Encrypt your wallet: Go to "Settings" and then click on "Encrypt Wallet". You will be asked to insert a pass phrase/password. Choose a lengthy and complex one. Do not store this pass phrase/password on your computer write a journal with all your passwords for wallets and pools.

3. Back your wallet up on a USB key and make a copy of it on another USB Stick

4. Now wrap the back up USB key in aluminum foil and store it in a safe place. aluminum foil might help to protect it from any EMI or potential EMP. also place in a fire poof safe.

Finding Currency Client and Using USB Flash Drives

We highly recommend using a couple reliable 8 GB USB Flash Drives to store your Coin Wallets. Using one as a main use update, store, back up and a second or even a third one as copy back ups to store in a safe place. Below is a step by step process on coin wallets. Visit the Crypto Currency client main website that you would like to own. You can find them by performing a search online with a search engine by typing the name of the coin. NOTE: Make sure you only download from the main website of that currency!

1. Download wallet zip file to computer's "download files folder".
2. Put in 8 GB USB Flash Drive and Format it by Right Click on USB Drive and format   3. Go to Downloaded Folder. Right Click on Mouse and extract the currency's file to the USB Flash Drive. Go to the New Folder.
4. Locate the main file and double click on it to start updating the block-chain.   5. Update the "Receive Coins" section. Click on "Label" and edit the label to your name. 6. Lastly After the block-chain has been updated. Encrypt the pass phrase and it will ask if ok then restart; after you click yes. Restart and make sure update client to current blocks date.

Hot Wallet vs. Cold Storage

A 'hot wallet' refers to a coin wallet which is connected to the internet either by desktop computer or smart phone. Cold storage refers to wallets kept on devices not connected to the internet, like a USB thumb drive. Hot wallets are instantly available to the user, while cold storage wallets cannot be accessed or hacked into remotely over the web. Wallets can be made in three places - on your computer as an application, as a mobile app on your smart phone, or on the web, where it is stored by a third party.

Malware and keystroke loggers

However, a hacker using malware to track your keystrokes - and thus the passwords you enter while using your computer - could still steal your coins. Basic practice here is important: keep your antivirus software up-to-date. An alternative to storing your wallet on your own computer is the web-based wallet, such as Blockchain.info. These wallets function in a similar way except the encryption keys are stored on the service provider's server, rather than your own computer; these keys are encrypted and only accessible using your password. Online wallets also offer two-factor authentication, whereby any login attempt by you (or a potential thief) requires your password, plus access to your mobile phone which is sent a code to be entered while logging in. Keeping crypto-coins safe might sound like hard work, but given the dramatic rise value over the last 12 months, a few extra security stages will always be better than having your coins stolen with no way of getting them back.

Encrypting Wallet

Go to Currency Program and find and select "Settings" and then click on "Encrypt Wallet". You will be asked to insert a pass phrase/password. Choose a lengthy and complex one. Do not store this pass phrase/password on your computer write a journal with all your passwords for wallets and pools.

NOTE: Make sure you write down your pass phrase or you'll loose all of your items after its locked. don't forget it. Always back up your wallet after any updates and payouts. NOTE: Make sure you write down your pass phrase or you'll loose all of your items after its locked. don't forget it. Back your wallet up on a USB key and make a copy of it on another USB Stick and wrap the back up USB key in aluminum foil place and store it in a safe place. aluminum foil might help to protect it from any EMI or potential EMP. also place in a fire poof safe.

Secure Internet Wallets

Another way of protection is to use a company who will back up your currency with internet protected server services. Coinbase.com is based in San Francisco, CA. and is committed to making bit coin secure and easy to use. The Company was founded in June of 2012, Coinbase is a bit coin wallet and platform where 809,000 consumer wallets, 20,000 merchants transact with the new digital currency bit coin and U.S. bank integration.

Password Strength Suggestions

Brute-force password cracking has come a long way. A password including capitals, numbers, and special characters with a length of 8 characters can be trivially solved now. The recommended length is at least 12 characters long. You can also use a multi-word password and there are techniques to increase the strength of your passwords without sacrificing usability. However, simply using dictionary words is also insecure as it opens you up to a dictionary attack. If you use dictionary words, be sure to include random symbols and numbers in the mix as well. If you use key files in addition to a password, it is unlikely that your encrypted file can ever be cracked using brute-force methods, even when even a 12 character password might be too short. Make sure you pick at least one character in each group:

Lowercase: abcdefghijklmnopqrstuvwxyz

Uppercase: ABCDEFGHIJKLMNOPQRSTUVWXYZ

Number: 1234567890

Symbol: `~!@#$%^&*()-_=+\|[{]};:'",<.>/? (space)

Amount of Characters: < 9 char = unsuitable for use

09 char = insecure

10 char = low security

11 char = medium security

12 char = good security (good enough for your wallet)

13 char = very good, enough for anything.

What are Mining Pools?

In the context of cryptocurrency mining, a mining pool is the pooling of resources by miners, who share their processing power over a network, to split the reward equally, according to the amount of work they contributed to solving a block.

https://en.bitcoin.it/wiki/Comparison_of_mining_pools

Registering, Setup, Account, Workers and Payout

1. Create account. Register or login if you already have account.

2. Create a worker that will be used by the miner to login.

3. Configure your miner

4. Create an address to receive payments. Download the client and update block chain. Install the Cypto Currency Wallet to USB. Generate a new address and input it on your account page to receive payments.

5. CG Miner settings

Don't set intensity too high, I=13 is standard and safest. Higher intensity takes more GPU RAM. Check for hardware errors in cgminer (HW). HW=0 is good, otherwise lower intensity. Set shaders according to the readme (or look at your graphic cards specifications). Cgminer uses this value at first run to calculate thread-concurrency.

Large Vs Small Hash Rate Pools

Small Pools will give out extra bonuses as an extra to have you mine with them. Special prizes and bonus for toughie block finders. "For every block > 200% you get extra for every 100%" or "Block Finders Get Extra". Large Pools will have more computers hashing and getting out more you payout will be based on your KW/s hash percentages for payout versus the others in the pool. Large Pools are more stable and tend to payout hourly instead of daily.

Multi Pools Vs Currency Only Pools

Multipools change to the very next best payout and lowest hash rate. These pools payout hourly or when they switch to the other currencies. Cons: You'll need a wallet for every coin currency the pool mines. it could be 10 wallets. the other con is that; if you want a specific coin currency you'll not be happy when it changes to the other ones as they do often. Cypto Currency Pools stay on the same currency. Obviously if you want that coin go to a non multi pool. if you want a lot of other coins and not have to switch the cgminer when you feel a tingle then use a multi pool.

Cryptocurrency Mining Profitability

Crypto currencies are being compared to Bitcoin to determine if a given crypto currency is more profitable to mine than Bitcoin based on the hash rate information provided. The current profitability information displayed is based on a statistical calculation using the values entered and does not account for difficulty and exchange rate fluctuations, stale/reject/orphan rates, a pool's efficiency, and pool fees. Your individual profitability may vary.

www.coinwarz.com/miningprofitability

Mining Pool Reward Types

CPPSRB - Capped Pay Per Share with Recent Backpay.

DGM - Double Geometric Method. A hybrid between PPLNS and Geometric reward types that enables to operator to absorb some of the variance risk. Operator receives portion of payout on short rounds and returns it on longer rounds to normalize payments.

ESMPPS - Equalized Shared Maximum Pay Per Share. Like SMPPS, but equalizes payments fairly among all those who are owed.

POT - Pay On Target. A high variance PPS variant that pays on the difficulty of work returned to pool rather than the difficulty of work served by pool.

PPLNS - Pay Per Last N Shares. Similar to proportional, but instead of looking at the number of shares in the round, instead looks at the last N shares, regardless of round boundaries.

PPLNSG - Pay Per Last N Groups (or shifts). Similar to PPLNS, but shares are grouped into "shifts" which are paid as a whole.

PPS - Pay Per Share. Each submitted share is worth certain amoutripnt of BC. Since finding a block requires current difficulty shares on average, a PPS method with 0% fee would be 12.5 BTC divided by current difficulty. It is risky for pool operators, hence the fee is highest.

Prop. - Proportional. When block is found, the reward is distributed among all workers proportionally to how much shares each of them has found.

RSMPPS - Recent Shared Maximum Pay Per Share. Like SMPPS, but system aims to prioritize the most recent miners first.

Score - Score based system: a proportional reward, but weighed by time submitted. Each submitted share is worth more in the function of time t since start of current round. For each share score is updated by: score += exp(t/C). Rewards are calculated proportionally to scores (and not to shares). (at slush's pool C=300 seconds, and every hour scores are normalized)

SMPPS - Shared Maximum Pay Per Share. Like Pay Per Share, but never pays more than the pool earns.

FPPS - Full Pay Per Share. Similar to PPS，but not only divide regular block reward (12.5 BTC for now) but also some of the transaction fees. Calculate a standard transaction fee within a certain period and distribute it to miners according to their hash power contributions in the pool. It will increase the miners' earnings by sharing some of the transaction fees.

Building a Profitable Mining Computer

GPU's: AMD Rx 470/480 Rx 570/580, AMD R9 range, HD 7990 / 7950 if used cards are available, try to get them from a gamer instead of a miner, with a warranty if possible. Nvidia, look at the 1060 / 1070 / 1080 series cards. GPU's based on hashrate, power requirements and price.

( ) 1 - Windows 7 64 or Windows 10 64

( ) 1 - Corsair Computer Case (Large Size)

( ) 1 - ASUS 64 Bit 990FX R2.0 Motherboard

( ) 1 - AMD 3.4 MHz 4 Quad 8 MB w/ fan

( ) 2 - 4 GB = 8 GB Ram - 1600 Mhz

( ) 1 - 1 TB 64 Bit Hard Drive Western Digital

( ) 1 - Cooler Master Silent Pro Gold 1200 w

( ) 2-4 - R90280X, XFX AMD GPU

( ) 1-2 - Riser Extension

( ) 1 - Good Monitor

( ) 1 - ASUS DVD Player

( ) 2-4 - 8 GB USB Flash Drives

( ) 4 - 12db fans

(   ) 1 Surge Protector

Lets Mine! CG Miner Mining Software Setup Online Software Downloads

Download the Video GPU Software
AMD Catalyst 13.2   Type: Url
http://sites.amd.com/us/game/downloads/Pages/radeon_win8-64.aspx

Download the GPU Hashing Software
CG Miner 3.7.2 Type: Url

http://ck.kolivas.org/apps/cgminer/3.7

Getting Started: Command. Copying Code in input box.
Scrypt Command Line Code:
(3) XFX AMD Raidon R90 280X Run @ 80 degrees and 3100 rpm : 720 -750 KH/s each

This tunes the optimal size of work that scrypt can do. It is internally tuned to the highest reasonable multiple of shaders that it can allocate on your GPU ie. --thread-concurrency XXXX
Copy Code Below and Paste into Shortcut link for CGminer Program :

C:\cgminer-3.7.2-windows\cgminer.exe -o "stratum+tcp://address":"portnumber" -u username."yourworkername" -p "password" --scrypt -I 13 -g 2 -w 256 --lookup-gap 2 --thread-concurrency 8192 --gpu-engine 1050 --gpu-memclock 1500 --no-submit-stale

^ Copy Above Code and Paste into CGminer's Shortcut on Desktop. Right Click and Click on "Properties" Then Paste into "Target" Window.

1. First Thing is to Configure in Windows. Start Menu (Run > CMD) and then copy paste this:

setx GPU_MAX_ALLOC_PERCENT 100
setx GPU_USE_SYNC_OBJECTS 1

2. Press Enter
3. Restart Computer   (part two)

1. Download version CGminer 3.7.2 (Not Higher Version) Url: http://ck.kolivas.org/apps/cgminer/3.7 or search " cgminer 3.7.2 "
2. Install to C Drive. C:\cgminer-3.7.2-windows\cgminer.exe
3. Open your Notepad or Word Program and Copy then Paste:

C:\cgminer-3.7.2-windows\cgminer.exe -o "stratum+tcp://address":"portnumber" -u username."yourworkername" -p "password" --scrypt -l 13 -g 2 -w 256 --lookup-gap 2 --thread-concurrency 8192 --gpu-engine 1050 --gpu-memclock 1500 --no-submit-stale

4. Edit Scrypt Code with Stratum Address and Port Number, User Name.Worker Name and Password.
5. Select All, Copy and Minimize Program.
6. Right Click on the CGminer Program, and Place a "Short Cut Link" to your Computers Desk Top.

7. Go to Desk Top. Right Click on the Shortcut of CGminer you just placed there. Copy and Paste Scrypt Code.
8. Start CGminer. You should be Mining!

Miner Scrypt Samples Used

--scrypt --worksize 256 --intensity 13 --gpu-threads 1 --thread-concurrency 8192 --lookup-gap 2 --gpu-engine 1155 --gpu-memclock 1500 --gpu-powertune 20 --no-submit-stale -o stratum+tcp://mine-doge.cryptoculture.net:22555 -u username.1 -p x
C:\cgminer-3.7.2-windows\cgminer.exe -o stratum+tcp://west1.us.stratum.dedicatedpool.com:3342 -u username.1 -p x --scrypt -I 13 -g 2 -w 512 --lookup-gap 2 --thread-concurrency 8192 --gpu-engine 1050 --gpu-memclock 1500 --gpu-powertune 20 --no-submit-stale

C:\cgminer-3.7.2-windows\cgminer.exe -o stratum+tcp://stratum-eu.dgb.luckyminers.com:3332 -u username.1 -p x --scrypt -I 13 -g 2 -w 512 --lookup-gap 2 --thread-concurrency 8192 --gpu-engine 1050 --gpu-memclock 1500 --gpu-powertune 20 --no-submit-stale

C:\Users\Miner001\Desktop\cgminer-3.7.2-windows\cgminer.exe --scrypt -o stratum+tcp://tag.cryptominer.net:3359 -u ogondenske.tagdigg -p x -I 13 -g 2 -w 512 --thread-concurrency 8000 --gpu-engine 1025 --gpu-memclock 1500

Morning
C:\Users\Miner001\Desktop\cgminer-3.7.2-windows\cgminer.exe --scrypt --thread-concurrency 6000 --gpu-engine 1000 --gpu-memclock 1500 -I 13 -g 2 -w 512 -o stratum+tcp://tag.cryptominer.net:3359 -u username.tagdigg -p x

Mid Day
C:\Users\Miner001\Desktop\cgminer-3.7.2-windows\cgminer.exe --scrypt --thread-concurrency 8000 --gpu-engine 1025 --gpu-memclock 1500 -I 13 -o stratum+tcp://tag.cryptominer.net:3359 -u username.tagdigg -p x

Cold Day Maxium
C:\Users\Miner001\Desktop\cgminer-3.7.2-windows\cgminer.exe --scrypt --thread-concurrency 8500 --gpu-engine 1025 --gpu-memclock 1500 -I 13 -o stratum+tcp://tag.cryptominer.net:3359 -u username.tagdigg -p x

Quick Troubleshooting Guide

CGminer Crashes or Doesn't Start
- Make sure you set intensity to 13 as a starting point and increase gradually for better hash rates.
- Use a SCRYPT miner because there are two versions of GUIMiner, one for SCRYPT and one for SHA.
- Run the program with the code --scrypt and --thread-concurrency "number" ?
- Have the correct video card drivers installed and the maximum thread-concurrency arguments are set correctly.
- Disable any sleep settings and automatic virus scanning.
- Using the correct username that you have set in the pool under workers so you get paid.
-u "username."yourworkername" -p "x"
(password for miners are usually "x")

Computer is freezing
- Lower the Hash Intensity, and lower the Over Clock Settings

Computer is shutting down randomly
- Make sure video card is below 90C
- Make sure your power supply can support the voltage

Can I use Bitcoin ASIC miners to mine for other Cypto Currency?
No, it's not possible. They use entirely different hashing algorithms. GPU is the only way right now.

Can I use the same worker name and password for various computers?
Yes, though using different workers helps you keep better track of your mining performance.

Why doesn't my hash rate report the same on the pool dashboard?

The way pool mining works, it has no way of knowing the exact hash rate. Instead it will estimate based on how frequently your shares are submitted.

CG Miner says it is running my GPU but I am not getting any shares?

You are running a unsupported version of CG Miner (3.8.x and higher is not supported)
You are running CG Miner without the --scrypt argument
Your command line is wrong, it should look like this.

How can I tell if my mining rig is earning anything?

Once you have your program set up and running, watch for ACCEPTED shares. Accepted shares are what count towards your payout. Is it normal to get Rejected shares?

Is it better to run my computer hardwired to the internet or wireless?

Wireless may cause high latency issues which would trickle to performance issues. If possible, hardwire your rig for best performance.

ETC Mining. Information and Setup

This is "proof-of-work," which means the computer which discovered the correct nonce must've actually done the work (i.e., used computing power to run the hashing algorithm) to arrive at that value. The miner that finds the correct nonce is then awarded the block, receives 5 ether, and the process then begins anew in a cycle that recurs about every 12 seconds.
https://www.genesis-mining.com/

If you're new to mining Ethereum, this covers all the important facts. Let's start with some short answers to common questions about Ethereum mining:

Why should I mine Ethereum tokens (aka ether or ETH)?
doesn't mining Ether take up a lot of electricity?
If done properly, more money is earned by selling mined ETH than is spent on electricity. In other words, it's profitable! You can check out the profitability with our Ethereum mining calculator.

Can I mine with my CPU (Personal computer's processor) instead of an expensive graphics card (GPU)? GPUs are so much faster that CPU-mining is no longer profitable or worthwhile. Even entry-level GPUs are about 200 times faster than CPUs for mining purposes.

What's the best GPU to use for getting the most ETH for the least electricity? AMD cards tend to edge out similarly-priced NVidia cards in terms of efficiency.

Why point your GPU towards a mining pool as opposed to solo-mining? Unless you throw a fortune into mining hardware, your odds of generating ETH on your own are low. Pool-mining allow you to earn ETH in a regular and predictable way.

How do I get started with mining Ethereum?
If you've got a suitable GPU with at least 3GB RAM

What are the OS requirements for mining?
Windows 10 (make sure it's 64 bit).

The Ethereum Mist wallet is not sync'ing for me, can I use any Eth wallet address for mining? You can use any ETH wallet address for mining, but some exchanges do not allow mining or do not allow very small deposits so double check with the site if mining directly to a web-deposit address. A good alternative to downloading the full Mist wallet and Ethereum blockchain is MyEtherWallet.com, which still allows you to manage your Ether wallet address and maintain control of your private keys which is important for security and/or wallet backup and restoration if needed.

What are system requirements for the Mining Rig?
There could be a very lengthy post on all the hardware requirements and considerations, but to cover the important things at a high level, here are some primary considerations. Your Windows 10 OS should be a 64 bit installation – You want to get a motherboard with enough PCI-E slots to support the number of cards you are running. If using more than one GPU, you'll want to get a powered pci-e riser for each additional GPU For Power Supplies, you want to double check that your PSU has enough connections to support the number of GPU's you are running and enough overall wattage to support your total system power draw (and to give yourself some buffer of at least 10-15%). A helpful site for identifying how many 6 or 8 pin PCI-E power connections your GPU will require is here (Realhardtechx.com) and to get a sense of your overall system power draw, this is a good power consumption calculator (outervision). Pro Tip: if building multiple rigs stick with the same brand PSU as you can use extra cables on your other systems if needed (e.g. I use only EVGA G2 PSU's so if I have extra VGA, sata or molex cables from one build I can use them on another build).

You want to get a simple low end CPU and at least 4GB of RAM

Tip: make sure your motherboard, CPU and RAM are compatible (i.e. LGA 1151 motherboards need an 1151 socket CPU, and DDR4 RAM / LGA 1150 motherboards need an 1150 CPU and DDR3 RAM) – Don't forget a power button! Pick up a simple PC power button switch which connects onto the headers of the motherboard so you can turn your system on/off – A standard keyboard, mouse and monitor are needed. If managing your rig remotely (not covered here in this beginner guide) you will want to get a headless hdmi dummy plug to plug into your rig so it boots into Windows properly for remote access.

What are the other options for mining Ethereum like with specialized ASIC hardware, gaming laptops, or Virtualized environments? As long as your system meets the general requirements and has at least one GPU with at least 3GB of RAM, you can mine Ethereum. Some Gaming laptops do have high end cards, but with the considerable heat generated from mining there could be other impacts to your laptop so it's best to go with a desktop build. Virtualized environments that you can rent usually do not have enough powerful dedicated GPU in them, or are simply not profitable if they do. There are currently no ASICs for Ethereum (as it is designed to be an "ASIC Resistant" Proof Of Work hashing algorithim, so if you see ads for one – RUN. ASIC's are still profitable for mining some coins (Bitcoin, Dash and Litecoin), but for home built Mining Rigs, Ethereum and other altcoins are still profitable to mine (whereas Bitcoin is not profitable on a home pc – even with many powerful GPU's do the Bitcoin ASIC technology available).

Building a large ETH position now, in the Proof of Work mining phase, will enable you to earn interest on your holdings when Ethereum switches to a Proof of Stake If you believe in the Ethereum concept you can support and gain voice in the Ethereum network through mining. Some of the above terms in bold probably require further clarification for cryptocurrency newcomers. Let's start with the Ethereum blockchain; the distributed digital ledger which you actually mine. Ethereum Blockchain Blocks are identified by their "height," starting from 0 and incrementing sequentially until the current block. Here's how the mining process serves to create, verify and record blocks: Miners listen for transactions over the network and amass all they consider valid (in terms of fees, code and the accounting history of who controls which coins) into blocks. Miners expend electricity hashing that block with the processing power of their GPU(s). A successful hash result produces produce a unique Proof of Work (PoW) proving that the miner worked on that block. If the rest of the network accepts the hashed block as valid, the block becomes part of the permanent consensus on valid transactions, known as the blockchain. The miner receives 5 ETH plus all transaction and code-processing fees (aka gas) contained in their block, plus a possible bonus for any uncles they include. How Ethereum's Blockchain Differs from Bitcoin's Ethereum uses a different hashing algorithm to Bitcoin, which makes it incompatible with the special hashing hardware (ASICs) developed for Bitcoin mining. Ethereum's algorithm is known as Ethash. It's a memory-hard algorithm; meaning it's designed to resist the development of Ethereum-mining ASICs.

Instead, Ethash is deliberately best-suited to GPU-mining. Hashrate, Difficulty and Price Total network hashrate has been climbing rapidly since Q2 2016.

Questions and Answers

What is Bitcoin? It's a decentralized digital currency

Why Use Bitcoin? It's fast, cheap to use, and secure

Who is Satoshi Nakamoto? The founder of bitcoin

What is the Difference Between Dogecoin, Litecoin and Bitcoin? It's the silver parts to bitcoin's gold

What is Blockchain Technology? A system of distributed data and logic

How Does Blockchain Technology Work? Cryptographic keys, distributed networks and network servicing protocols

What Can a Blockchain Do? Identity, recordkeeping, smart contracts and more

What is a Distributed Ledger? A dynamic, independently maintained database

What is the Difference Between a Blockchain and a Database? It begins with architectural and administrative decisions

Why Use a Blockchain? To manage and secure digital relationships as part of a system of record.

What is Ethereum? A blockchain application platform and 'world computer'

What is Ether? The 'fuel' of the ethereum network

Who Created Ethereum? Vitalik Buterin

What is a Decentralized Application? A distributed 'smart contract' system

What is a DAO? A 'decentralized autonomous organization'

How Do Ethereum Smart Contracts Work? Code, transaction fees and 'gas'

How Will Ethereum Scale? 'Sharding' and 'off-chain' transactions.

Glossary and Definitions

Block - A block is what miners try to complete to receive coin rewards. They contain a list of transactions that occur on the network, as well as information about where the transactions took place in the block chain, and other information describing the block.

Block Reward - When a block is found and completed, and confirmed by the network, there is a block reward that the founder receives.

Dig – Dig is the term used in the client to refer to mining coins. Running a program, your computer will attempt to solve complicated math problems, and if you are successful at solving them, and it is confirmed by the rest of the network, you will be rewarded with a block reward.

Difficulty - A number that represents how difficult it is to find and complete a block. It is computed by the number total mining power that all the miners on the network are using. The more people with good hardware that mine, the harder it is to get coins.

Client – This is the software you download that contains the coin wallet and allows you to perform basic coin operations like sending and receiving coins.

Mining Pool - A mining pool is a group of miners who work together to find and complete a block. Mining in a group makes it much more consistent for miners to get rewarded for block finding, as coins are split among the mining pool when the block is found, completed and confirmed by the network.

Orphaned Block - An orphaned block is a block that has been mined but has been rejected by the network. This occurs because another block was confirmed by the network that had the same transactions. Because multiple miners may be competing to find a block and finish it before the others, the one to be finished and confirmed by others on the network will be considered valid while any others that were being completed will considered invalid or orphaned. Orphans do not reward the finders with any coins.

Private Key (Wallet) – A private key is used to show proof that you own a public address, and any coins that are assigned to it. In the wallet, these are usually hidden and can only be retrieved through special commands. If you don't have a backup of your wallet and don't have the private keys, there is no way for you to retrieve any funds that you had in your wallet. So make sure you backup your wallet!

Public Key (Wallet) – A wallet public key is the public address that can be used to receive coins, is used in transactions, and is otherwise used to "get paid". Anyone can view the balance or send coins to a public key. But no one can claim ownership of the public key without the private key.

Wallet – A wallet is a collection of public and private keys that are used to send and receive coins. They can be password protected and backed up.

Multi-Coin Exchanges

Where to Buy Cryptocurrency? Ranging from BTMs (Bitcoin ATMs), embassies, and exchanges, cryptocurrencies can be bought and traded at multiple locations worldwide.Cryptocurrency exchanges are websites where you can buy, sell, or exchange cryptocurrencies for other digital currencies or traditional currencies such as US dollars or Euro.

Use the following links : When you sign up using your referral code you'll get 10% off discount on all trading fees for 6 months. Signup page URL: www.gate.io/signup/129542

- BTC-E
- LitecoinLocal
- Crypto-Trade

Market Data and Tools

Crypto Market Cap (http://www.cryptomarketcap.com)

Cryptocoin Charts (http://www.cryptocoincharts.org)

Bitcoin Analytics (http://www.bitcoin-analytics.com)

Cryptocompare (http://www.cyrptocompare.com)

Meta Trader 4 (http://www.metatrader4.com)

Clark Moody Data (http://www.bitcoin.clarkmoody.com)

Bitcoinity (http://www.bitcoinity.org/markets)

Coin Warz (http://www.coinwarz.com)

News Sources

CoinTrader (http://www.coin-trader.com)

References

http://wikipedia.org the free encyclopedia,

http://www.ck.kolivas.org/apps/cgminer/3.7

http://www.coingecko.com/en/price_calculator

http://www.coinwarz.com/miningprofitability

http://en.bitcoin.it/wiki/Comparison_of_mining_pools

Computer Miner Computer Build List

(   ) 1 - Windows 7 64 (is best)

(   ) 1 - Corsair Computer Case (Large Size)

(   ) 1 - ASUS 64 Bit 990FX R2.0 Motherboard

(   ) 1 - AMD 3.4 MHz 4 Quad 8 MB w/ fan

(   ) 2 - 4 GB = 8 GB Ram - 1600 Mhz

(   ) 1 - 1 TB 64 Bit Hard Drive Western Digital

(   ) 1 - Cooler Master Silent Pro Gold 1200 w

(   ) 2-4 - R90280X, XFX AMD GPU

(   ) 1-2 - Riser Extension

(   ) 1 - Good Monitor

(   ) 1 - ASUS DVD Player

(   ) 2-4 - 8 GB USB Flash Drives

(   ) 4 - 12db fans

( ) 1 Surge Protector

Computer Miner Computer Build List

( ) 1 - Windows 7 64 or Windows 10 64

( ) 1 - Corsair Computer Case (Large Size)

( ) 1 - ASUS 64 Bit 990FX R2.0 Motherboard

( ) 1 - AMD 3.4 MHz 4 Quad 8 MB w/ fan

( ) 2 - 4 GB = 8 GB Ram - 1600 Mhz

( ) 1 - 1 TB 64 Bit Hard Drive Western Digital

( ) 1 - Cooler Master Silent Pro Gold 1200 w

( ) 2-4 - R90280X, XFX AMD GPU

( ) 1-2 - Riser Extension

( ) 1 - Good Monitor

( ) 1 - ASUS DVD Player

( ) 2-4 - 8 GB USB Flash Drives

( ) 4 - 12db fans

( ) 1 Surge Protector

Version 1.02 DEC 2017

www.ingramcontent.com/pod-product-compliance
Lightning Source LLC
LaVergne TN
LVHW052125070326
832902LV00038B/3940